Kraken

Anna (Span) Streatfeild

BookLeaf Publishing

Presentation by *BookLeaf Publishing*

Web: www.bookleafpub.com

E-mail: info@bookleafpub.com

ISBN: 978-93-95950-23-7

First edition 2022

DEDICATION

For Span,

Be kind.

ACKNOWLEDGEMENT

Big thanks to my Brother Nomis for blindly
funding this pursuit,
and to the rest of my family for your relentless
support and love.

PREFACE

A lot of this poetry is a response to "First We Make the Beast Beautiful" A book by Sarah Wilson that had a beautiful cover and wonderful premise, but impractical and condescending advice, at least for me at the time (an undiagnosed Autistic) A book in which I furiously responded with pencil written notes in the margins. A very effective book, which inspired me to create.

My Octopus

In regards to my anxiety; I feel kinda stuck in a
rut
Not as chasmic as the last one but,
a shallow edge. That I seem to be
constantly lapping up against.

I have a tidal push and pull
some waves splash over the wall
and into.... confidence?
Sometimes.

But the ocean drags back into itself.
This is why I find relationships
so difficult. I don't want others
to get trapped in my riptide.

I don't want them to get pulled
so far out into me, and my mental illness
that they get beaten by octopus
and swallowed by kraken.

This, is an interesting metaphor.
I like it because I fear the ocean,
while also being inspired by it.

If (simile) I, am the Ocean

then my childhood dreams of becoming a
marine biologist (I never wanted to be a
mermaid)
have come true.

I research. I study. I experiment.
And mostly the ocean grinds me down.
Some days I am the mountain range.
Some days I am the sand.

My sense of self isn't just the anxiety
of the ocean. I am the whole ecosystem.
But octopuses, have you seen those
beautiful beasts?

Those are Alien. Those I can
identify as 'other' My octopus are
intrusive thoughts I can train to swim
by my side!

but sometimes,
this doesn't help.

Right now My octopus is my bad mood.
My octopus is an unfinished creation.
My octopus, is that I'm constantly, exhausted.

My Octopus is that positive thinking
is brain washing and I know

that I am manipulating myself away
from the #truth

My Octopus is that I wrote a poem.
Yesterday.
So much to live up to.
My octopus is that I am in pain.

I am tired. But my Octopus isn't.
There are tentacles everywhere.
Suctioning all over the room.
Hitting me in the face.

My Octopus leaves scars.
My Octopus is spiralling.
My Octopus is the Kraken.
My Octopus, is a disability.

I am going to push through the tentacles
and I am going to thrive irregardless
of whether My Octopus is smothering me,
Or swimming by my side.

My Octopus (continued)

My Octopus is snaking it's tentacles
underneath my skin. It is circling
my ribcage. Forcing it's way between
my muscles and poking at my vitals.

My octopus doesn't like my lungs.
It feels threatened by the ease at which
they continue to inhale.... exhale...
My Octopus hates that my brain watches my
lungs.

Inhale.... Exhale....
My Octopus is a jealous cephalopod.
It doesn't like being ignored, or controlled,
or left out.
Breathe in... Breathe out...
My Octopus doesn't listen to discipline.

My Octopus is rage, silent bottling
Restrictive Rage that grips fiercely
at my existence and leaves
sucker marks on my soul.

When my Octopus is angry,
it evolves blue rings.

Poisoning me. Poisoning everything
I touch.

But my Octopus is sneaky.
You see it's very good at hiding.
When people look at me, they cannot
see the tentacles.

They don't notice my pain.
My octopus has an ever changing façade.
My octopus sounds like
"I'm good thanks, and you?"

My octopus wears protective gear
and carries a clipboard.
My octopus had no access limits.
It will walk in anywhere at any time.

But the thing about my octopus
you see, is that it is ever present. Omnipresent.
All Hours. 24/7
Inescapable.

I actively imagine My Octopus occasionally.
It's becoming a coping mechanism now.
Writing this poetry is making
My Octopus squirm.

It's making it listen.

It's making it fear me.
You hear this, Octopus?
Our tides are turning! Heel.

You will swim by my side! Heel!
You will swim by my side, Heel.
You will swim by my side Heel.
I am asking you, to Heal.

Anxious

When I say I am anxious,
It sounds like, it stands alone
Like it's just one thing.
But Anxiety is a plural.

It's not just nerves
It's not just spiralling thoughts, it's not just
shaky hands and an unsteady
heartbeat

It's not telling yourself to maintain eye contact.
Maintain eye contact
Maintain eye contact!
Why can't you maintain eye contact!?

Anxiety is like a novel.
You might only have one book.
But it will access you, word by frightening
word
Only all the words come at you at once.

Every sentence of the book its shouted at you
simultaneously, repeatedly, forever..
there are no rests for chapters or cut scenes.
There are no page numbers.

And you might be hearing more than one book.
Each book a different diagnosis.

Anxiety

You can have depression without having
Anxiety
You can have OCD without having Anxiety
You can have a life without having Anxiety.
But I don't know how.

When I say I can't come because
my anxiety is playing up;
You hear " I'm feeling anxious about this"
You hear " I'm too lazy"
You hear "I don't want to"
You hear that I am flaking again.

Here is what you don't hear:
My heartbeat behind my eyes.
Is that a snake?
Of course it's not a snake. What are you insane?
But what if it is? Just check.

I already have.
Check again.
I just did!
Again.
Stop it.
Check it!

Stop it!
Why?? Why do you have to stop your own thoughts? Why aren't you even capable of thinking? Everyone else can think. Even babies.
You should cry now.

Why are you crying?
Stop it.
Nobody else is crying.
Stop it.

What you don't hear, is my fists clenched into my eyeballs
pressing against my heartbeat.

You don't hear the constant unease in my stomach
You don't hear my flesh, bruised by my own hand.
You don't hear the screaming

You don't hear the multitudes of ways I can tell myself that I'm worthless.
You don't hear the fight I have with those thoughts.
You don't hear the replies back.

My anxiety is wittier than I am.

You don't hear how long it's been
since I've left my house, since I've showered.
Since I've forgotten to breathe.

So hear me when I say I am anxious.
for I am simply telling the truth.

My Octopus ((continued))

My Octopus doesn't quite believe I am doing this.
My octopus doesn't even care what this is.

It wraps it's tentacles around my neck,
around my ribs. Around my hurt.

Infiltrating and constricting
my entire being with fear.

My octopus thinks that
if I just stand still
if I just stop treading water
if I just let myself sink

Then I won't have to struggle anymore.

This Poem Is Not About Love

I don't remember actually believing
in Santa Claus
That is to say I never had that
earth shattering realisation that
grown ups lie.
Especially about everything fun.
Everything fun is a game.
A game like Netball.
Not that netball itself was fun,
but the game was.
I remember in primary school
I got a trophy for playing netball.
That didn't mean I was any good at it,
but it was fun to hold the award
and play along.

Just because I never believed in fairies
doesn't make them any less real.

Christmas is still magical.
It's beautiful.
People are at least trying to be happier.
Even the corporations are playing along.

I do remember moments in my childhood
looking for angels in the clouds and
fairy doors at the bottom of the garden
with grownups, and wondering
If they actually were... insane?
If they were disappointed
to learn that it was a notch in the tree
where a branch used to be?

I wondered not if the world of adults
were liars, instead I feared for their sanity.
It doesn't matter if it's real or not,
what matters is that you look anyway!

What matters is being open
to the possibility
what matters is that you don't ruin the game.

I don't believe in fairies.

The Cure

Stop Complaining
Push your boundaries
Just don't worry about it.
Breathe deeply
Meditate
Do yoga
Exercise
Eat healthy
Get 8 hours of sleep
Travel
Believe in something greater than yourself
Over articulate your words
Stop being sad
Get angry
Make new friends
Be interested in something, anything
But no, not that.
Write
Read
Do something
Get excited
Fake it till you make it
Just keep swimming
Did you forget to breathe?
Calm down.

Take deep breaths
Realise
There is no cure
Acknowledge your complaints
Accept you have boundaries
Try not to worry about how
much you are worrying.
Breathe deeply
Try meditation. It's okay if its not for you
Try Yoga.   It's okay if it's not for you
Go outside
Make thought out choices about food.
Aim for 8 hours sleep
It doesn't matter if you go over or under.
Relax
Believe in yourself
Speak to someone, if you can.
Listen if they talk back.
Remember
It is okay to be sad.
It is okay, to be sad.

Understand

I am sure there are statistics you'd like to hear.
Reducing people into graphs
lives into numbers,
mental illness into
something you can understand

The voices in my head sound like a thousand
poets
whose names I haven't memorised but whose
words have helped carve out this personality
I've become.

You see I stand on the backs of giants.
I am the accumulation of other people's
creativity
I am a regurgitation of everything I've
consumed
we are all the absorption of what we consume
Of who we hang out with.
My inner voices are the biggest sponges
They change my accent to mimic
Those around me until I no longer
recognise the sounds of my own voice.

I want to punch every mirror I see.

Not because I hate my reflection,
but because I don't recognise her.

Simultaneously wanting to blend invisibly
into the background while desperately
trying to separate myself from society.

I am craving chocolate like air in a drowning
girl's lungs
I am bleeding like a snowstorm over Manhattan

There is something steadfast in the shaky grip
that anxiety has on my stomach

I don't think beauty could really exist without
sadness

Trace your fingers between my freckles
and share your hope with me.

Son,

I like magnolias
They are beautiful flowers
Tall Trees
They reach for the Sky and they
Spread their leaves proudly.
I'd like to name my theoretical son,
Magnolia
Some would say this is yet another reason why
I shouldn't have kids.
But hear me out. Magnolias have no obvious
gender
And by god boys can be beautiful.
Magnolias are large and bright and humble
and they, like all life on earth, are fleeting.

And so my boy, I want you to stand tall.
Shoulders squared
a gentle smile on your face
Throw shade for those who need it.
Provide shelter under your leaves
Quietly unfurl your petals while no one is
watching.
Shine bright regardless of the attention you
may or may not receive.
Be humble. Be proud. Be kind.

Reach for the heavens and remember
my dear boy
you, are temporary.

Dear Poetry

Like tears in the rain
a drop in the ocean
Like everything I want to say
has already been said before
a thousand times.
but this
Poetry,
This is why I feel heard when I listen
to you.

Anxiety (continued)

The thing about my Anxiety
is that it is attention seeking.
It hides behind my eyes until it leaks out
streaming down my face, in what looks,
from the outside, to be an unexpected manner,
I breathe.
I suck the tears back into their ducts and
I breathe.
and I voice the fact that I have a disorder
my voice cracks and my breathing is heavy
and the tears are back and I'm shaking.
It's controlling me again.
It feels loved when I am messy.
It feels sharp like razor blades pushing out
from underneath my skin.
Anxiety wants me to focus on it.
Relish in it.
Wallow in the frustrated misery that spirals
negativity into my soul.

Dear Poetry (continued)

I've missed you.
When I kiss you it isn't like lightning.
But when your hand brushes mine, I get tingles.
The butterflies in my heart get excited.
When we make eye contact and you call me
sunshine,
the rest of the world ceases to exist for a blissful
moment.

But kissing you is warm and moist and
desperately wants to be familiar.
Yet all I could think about was my glasses
pressing against your face.
You see kissing you isn't like what I've read
about in books.
I have no idea where my hands were.
I'm not sure if my eyes were open or closed.
I don't know if my leg popped.
Because apparently all these things are
important.
But to me, what's important is,
The way your shoulders relax as we talk
is the smirk on your face when I look away.
Is the sensitivity in the back of my neck
when you run your hands through your hair.

Your arms have become my sanctuary
and I hope I belong here.

exes

To my Ex-poet boyfriend
Is our happiness, stifling your creativity?
Don't worry.
You'll soon be miserable again.
When you realise the true sadness
Behind my eyes
When I laughed, when you said
That you'd honestly rather
Name your hypothetical son "Rex"
Than Magnolia.

To my Ex- boyfriend Poet.
I might be biased, but
I am very much of the opinion that
You wrote your best works,
Between my thighs.

Exhaustion is Temporary

I have this underlying lament
this despair for existence.
This Tired.
That rolls over lazily when someone
tries to say something motivational like
the idea that you've lost so much weight
So you're healthier now,
So you'll live so much longer.
and all I hear is your life is hard and you have to endure it.

I like words

I like words
I like carving them our of nothingness.
I get frustrated at times when my
mind creates poems faster than my
fingers can record them.

I have an anxiety disorder.
A hyperness that makes me restless.
That makes me unable to sleep.
That makes me lose focus when I'm halfway
through a sentence.

Do I think anxiety has ruined my life?
See that's an interesting question to answer
because honestly. I don't know a life
without it.
Anxiety is clever sometimes. It makes you think
it isn't real
that everyone feels this way
and you think that as your stomach churns
and your clammy hands won't stop shaking
and you grip the door handle too hard
and your heart is floundering at the back of your
throat

and you're imagining a thousand ways you could die,
to simply get out of visiting a friend.
a friend you like.
a friend you want to visit in
a place you know.
you wipe your hands on your pants.
and you focus on your breathing
and you walk out of that door anyways
because anxiety can also be a strong motivator.

And this is called recovering.

Because you can still breathe
and you are still standing
and you aren't still crying.
This is a victory.

Simple accomplishments become great triumphs,
and you have to see them this way.
Because anxiety will grind away at anything good.
You have to keep building the good up wherever you can.
Sometimes it's grinding creates a smooth beautiful surface, other times it leaves a chasmic void.

You see I like words.
I like the way the craft takes over itself.
Inventing new ways to say the same
old stories. New ways to express.
New ways to make things clear.
I like communication.
The idea that I can transfer my selected
thoughts into someone else's mind.
You can do this with words. With language.
You can do this with art. With music.
With creativity.
My thoughts are not images, my mind runs on
words
it churns with language .
The voices in my head are arguing.
They aren't playing piano, or colouring in.
They are talking.
Writing is me trying to find the most effective
way
of listening.

I hope I have the vocabulary to do myself
justice.

Things about me

My Relationship with my body.

The freckles on my chest.
The freckles on my chest, the freckles,
on my chest.

The way I steal other people's poetry
their structure, their accents.
I think if I was a poet, I would have nothing
original to say.

As I take a drag with my genius.
My genius who holds hands with depression.
My genius who flirts with anxiety,
but never commits.
My flaky, fake, thief, of a genius,
who taunts me with ideas but never follows
through.

The voices in my head sound like poets
sound like you.
Sound like angels weeping for their fallen
brother.
Sound like Satan hearing their agony

and constructing himself out of the hollowed
out
bones of their grief.
Constructing himself out of their desperation
and
loneliness tempting me into self criticism and
loathing.

Never do the voices in my head sound like me.

Sometimes my smile is shattered glass.
Reflecting a thousand times out but
never quite reaching my eyes.
Sometimes my smile is the laugh out loud
simplicity of pure joy.
Sometimes I am over saturated with gratitude
for the universe, and other times
I am personally victimised by the sunny
weather

So I build up my walls
brick by brick, stone by stone.
Grasping at your grief, clutching at your agony.
begging, borrowing and stealing
from your emotional wealth.
My foundation stone was happiness
My default expression, a smile.
But the universe has endless materials
to share and I pick and choose

the darkest, stickiest stones.
To protect, to hide myself.
My body is soft.
The brain is the softest, most vulnerable
tissue in the human body.
My Mind is the strongest part of me.
The most difficult to locate, the hardest,
to understand or control.

My relationship with my mind.
My relationship with my soul.
My relationship with my heart.

My relationship with my body.

The freckles in my eyes.
The freckles in my eyes, the freckles,
in my eyes.

Sleep

Lying in my bed at 11:30 in the morning
having only just woke up
I slept. I slept solidly
an unusual occurrence for one
such as anxious as I.

Except that I have been sleeping well
consistently recently and the thing that
stings about that is that
it doesn't help.

There are still solid lumps of darkness
behind my eyes.
There are still whispers in my ears.
My tears do not fall.

I keep my eyes closed
so that the outside world
looks the same as my inside one.

Exhaustion is temporary
I chant in the darkness
of my mindscape.
These bad days will end.

I let the sentiment wash over me.
It doesn't reach a truth.
Like water off a ducks back.
No amount of sleep is soaking in.

I am glad the night mares aren't gone.
The memories of their terrors are evidence
that I actually was asleep.

Not just lying here, with my eyes closed.
Wishing to cry.

I am sad.

I don't know how to process sad.
Sad is different to nihilistic,
Sad is different to grief
Sad is different to depression.
Sad, is not anxious.

Sad is soft. Sad is tender.
Sad isn't a raw open wound, Sad,
Sad is bruised. Sad doesn't clench it's teeth.
Sad doesn't hold back tears.

Sad is squelchy underfoot when downtrodden,
Sad is the beginnings of quicksand.
Sad breathes deep. Sad doesn't hyperventilate.
Sad plods on.

My Sadness manifests itself
in a dull ache behind my eyes
Like all good Storms,
this too shall pass.
I just have to wait out the storm and,
Be kind.

It's like God took my guardian angel, ripped her
wings off.
and now, here I am, standing in front of myself.

Start Slow

You see I didn't write this poem.
I have never written a poem.
My Anxiety does it for me.

I am but a vessel for anxiety to be poured out
of.
To be poured through.
I am fragile like glass.
One clumsy bump and I will be shattered

My anxiety flooding the room
and staining the carpet red like purple wine.
It never comes off. But also, like bruises.
The blood will recede.

The shards of myself will be
littered in that carpet.
Don't walk barefoot around me
for I will make you bleed.

Slowly
My pieces will crawl back together
into something that might once again
be able to hold something.

A hollow vessel that leaks now.
That has scars.
That starts slowly,
and bleeds poetry.

Pandemic

I think the worst part of this new normal
is the systemic ableism.

Facts have been changing at a rate
so fast that it's impossible for my
Autistic brain to keep up and adapt.

I'm hearing it's just like a flu.
If. IF you're young and triple vaxxed
If you're able bodied and of sound mind.
If you don't have pre-existing conditions.

But like, you know, "we'll" be fine.
we the majority.

For two years the government and societal
social pressure has been leaning into
keeping everyone safe.

And then suddenly the numbers jump
and the spike feels like a plateau
but I can't make that call because,
because it's changing

and I can't keep up.

But it's up to me.
It's on the individual now.
Do what makes you comfortable
but let me tell you, I've never been comfortable.

I haven't been comfortable in years.
Years before the Pandemic.
Years before the Bushfires.
Years before my back injury.
Years and years before being confused and
uncomfortable and disabled.

There was an element of respect
that I felt. I didn't know it was there
at the time but there was a fundamental
idea that society wanted me to survive.
And thrive.
With this new normal, there is no ideals.

I can't keep up with the ever changing rules
and societal pressures and expectations.
and I'm soo so trying to keep up.

So maybe I make my world smaller.
Maybe I make my world smaller, and maybe
that's okay.

Maybe I stay on the internet and

make my videos, maybe I use my indoor
exercise bike, maybe I picnic on the balcony,
and maybe I let my world become small
and maybe that's okay.

Maybe I don't check the numbers.
Maybe I don't sleep regular hours.
Maybe I drift so far from normal ,
that I don't have to keep up.

So far removed
from society that I no longer need to function
within it.
I can be societally adjacent

I can remove the pressure and the risk,
by removing myself from the equation.

How do you know there is anything out there?
The door is closed.

The Kraken

The difference is that
now I know I am my Octopus,
I can use that to my advantage.

When everything's too much and
relationships are full of misunderstandings
and the lights are too bright and there's a leaf
blower beneath my window (my greatest foe)

I can take those same tentacles and
wrap them tightly around myself,
deliberately.
I can just sink into the quiet, in the bottom of the
ocean
and I can weather the storm.

These Bad Days Will End.

And when they do, when
everything is a little less bright.
A little gentler and a little more bearable,
I can take those tentacles and harness
the power of my octopus to stand taller
than ever before. Using those relentless
suctioning blue rings to cling to my special
interest

and climb mountains.
To walk in the sand.
To swim the ocean.

You see having the knowledge
of truly knowing my octopus is part of myself,
something that's always been a sad tortured
part of myself, now gives me a sense of self
nurturing, self kindness and one way or another
its nice to have a semblance of self love.

My octopus cannot heal.
Cannot swim by my side.
It cannot slap me in the face
nor hold me in a restrictive embrace.
It cannot be Separate, or alien or Other.

It is a part of the whole ecosystem that makes up
who I am.
And my octopus makes me weaker sometimes.
Rendering me utterly exhausted and crying and
messy.
But my Octopus is also a great strength.
For sometimes I am unstoppable,
or at least very passionate and will
go to extreme lengths of being subjected
to being uncomfortable.

My octopus does not like society.

Society was not built for an Octopus.
If I were to show you my tentacles
You would outcast me, silently snickering
you'd feel unconsciously superior and
you would deem me other.
Make me feel alien.
but not anymore.

I am my Octopus and I am strengthening my spine,
bracing my limbs, I am existing irregardless of societies
expectations and pressure.
I, am dismantling preconceived ideas
of who I should be and becoming
whomever I am.

Who ever my octopus make me become.

I once wanted to be a marine biologist.
I am now my greatest master and my keenest student.
I know who I am.
Yet am constantly learning more about myself.
My octopus is revealing secrets
and showing me hidden strengths I assumed I'd never have

I am become Kraken

www.ingramcontent.com/pod-product-compliance
Lightning Source LLC
Chambersburg PA
CBHW051739130826
49812CB00033B/927
9789395950237